Contents

I have battered, gilded & gifted
thrice, my heart to the world.
All for lessons I still won't claim to know.

Battered

One Haiku

Was there ever one?
A rhyme or reason,
For all the power in your word.

Sights & sounds of scum

I couldn't hear my heart
beneath the continuous hum
of having all my nerves
pulled so far and strum.

I witnessed life set to be
bent to a will plain & miserly.
Lost to the multitudes
seemingly wanton
in search of an end that will better none.

Here, enveloped in your raucous litany,
unable to pluck the one from the many,
I question - when of your once,
do you cease to be?

All around me, legions of the said & done
with no pretence to live beyond their wretched sum;
Their hearts lost amidst
the sights & sounds of scum.

Two Haiku

When you shaped these wilful eyes;
Did you forget then,
they would witness the whole world?

To die is sincere.

Steps echo a cold preamble to coming winter.
It permeates the otherwise silent inference of continuity
I assent to with every step.

Around me, all of life goes quietly -
it lives regardless.
Down the promenade, a single tree
stands golden & brown against the dark.

When the summer heath faltered;
The birds deserted
and its' splendour was no longer needed,
it was returned to earth.

Now it stands in the midst of night!
All of it bold death & fell beauty.
Beside it, all is lifeless.

Houses, with their pale glow;
Concrete, with its' accented, unnatural angles
& me, in my commute.

How pretentious of us!
to carry on like this
when to die is so sincere.

Red Haiku

Curse the shadow of things you
have brought light upon.
They hold the scent of rot there.

Half a glass

I'm so very done with you
"half full" people.

It makes me wonder just how little
you could drown in;

that you'd deem yourself so easily quenched
with half a fucking glass.

Blue Haiku

I would hope to know one day,
life that may sustain
all you just could never bare.

Maledict

A curse upon me.
Thought, and thus brought to be.

How it pains me!
this insipid; infectious lethargy.
How it drains me!
this absolute lack of substance here.

Still - it shapes me.

I am corroded by fear.
Indexed in this malaise I breathe.
I am measured in lost dreams
and stolen sleep.

When the venom seeps,
it is sure to flood my chest.
On days like these,
silence may be best

lest I drown.

Malediction runs so very deep.

Gilded

And so we write

Words alone fail oh! so beautiful.

Bright & the golden

The hours; the nights; the seasons we burned away!
Far from the absent crowds,
in places no doubt could shroud
we willed to abandon time.

From the flames -
center to our circles -
danced streaks of light
to fill and frame the night

as bright & golden as we were.

Of what worth is the future
to hearts which,
with every breath,
refuse to fear death?

How very golden we were!

Still, in memory of us;
to celebrate past fires,
I stoke daily a new pyre -
That today may burn as bright.

Summer Rain

Those were dog days; unfit for flight.
In the haze of heat, young swallows were grounded
and neglected. Their cries - lost
beneath all of the worlds wants -
asked only for the simplest needs.

And I doubt that ever thence they spared a thought
for any who - unlike you - would not take heed.
Poor marauders who never knew
love in acknowledged pain or
remission in the broken.

But of one act they may still sing.
Or perhaps, they carry it silently in the wind,
as I have often evoked your strengths and faults
but no word was ever spoken of the lessons therein.

Yes, those were dog days; unfit for flight!
and in a seemingly unwitting way,
your affect was summer rain.

On the mantle

I've been pilling up rocks on the mantle
and they don't mean much,
not to me anyway.

I still collect them;
display them
and on days when I am silent and melancholy,
I admire them.

They come from different places I have visited,
loved & hated.
Some were gifts
and a good few have at some point
bruised skin & broken bone.

Still, I fancy them.
At this point, they make a significant collection,
though they don't mean much.
Not to me, anyway.
I sure don't envy the fool however,
who'll have to clear them up one day.

If I didn't know any better

A bed undone
and coffee warm
is nice.

If I didn't know any better,
I might have chalked love up
to simple comforts.

The heart is an aesthete

Passion will not stand to be lost to a humble stage!
At this, we are impressed deeply
a most thespian sense.

Every moment must be full;
every humour professed.

For to fail the tragedy is to inhabit a vacant scene -
a horror unequalled,
to a heart committed to, no audience,

but to hopes, instead,
of animating a lifeless set.

Over breakfast

It's early in the day
and we've been dragging on the morning
over breakfast.

There's a song on, about yesterdays,
like so many others.
But you sway a little to this one.

I watch you get ready,
kiss me
and tell me you'll miss me.

And I sit there,
knowing you'll come back.

Favour the lot

I take this much to be true -
and I've seen it confirmed more often than not,
in my life and the ones of those I once knew -
that what you give value to holds your lot.

And I know it comes out funny sometimes
in the things I do, or maybe fail to,
but I'd hope they wouldn't read as signs
that I should come to miss you.

Gifted

Not one destitute moment

The past has died a thousand times.

It left me to stagger on;
often shedding contingent ties.
And looking behind me there is nowhere the heart lies.

No place to return.

Everything I know
and every second spent
will become loving memories in tow.

Among them, not one destitute moment.

Yesterdays' strength encompassed its' fall
and before today deserts me,
I surrender it all.

Given to purpose

The road winds furiously down to my feet,
thence forth it extends but an inch
to where my shadow lay.

Its' end is fabled to grandeur but
having travelled so far and determinately for so long
I have dedicated myself to the path.

I am only a marauder made stagnant,
arrived at nothing.

Unrequited

I didn't want you
to always love me.

I wanted you
to love me now
then.

Art demands

Wherever it may reach,
every breath I've breathed
is but a concept to form.

As wind upon the sail,
so am I inexpressible.
Bellowing out intently yet inconsequential
but for the resisting canvas.

Billow out
and belie the immutable horizon.

Bear intent upon the page I've populated
with only concept to form.

The things we take

In love proclaimed and in exhausted -
maybe even lost - care, we have lived.

In every tear shed
and every smile shared

we have learned and -
more than understood -

we held life such as one
could never come to own,

in all the things we take
from one another.

Acceptance makes a gift

There are sounds of you.
There is warmth & dance.
I'd hate to presume,
but today must have been offered us.

There is something of home,
if only even an instance.
There is laughter where there might be pain.
Today must have offered us love.

Sympathy flowers

Consider the flower
plucked from its' prime,
placed and propped in wait
of the pain and prayers of those
who come before it to rest and pine
for a loss comparable only to itself.

Ponder - in being picked -
the sacrifice that it never understood
and could not have foreseen.
The life that it gave without choice
yet freely and without a fight.

Only in this! I know no man unlike it.
Though many act with volition
and other such many with spite,
they never understood their invaluable sacrifice.

To Caesar

To everyday,
my experience and my pain.
My ageing and all it can claim.
But not my obeisance.

To god,
my birth and what may ensue.
All my disdain, he may have it too.
But not my faith.

To Caesar,
my efforts and their gain.
My house and whatever fame.
But not my allegiance.

To the world,
all it may affect.
All the belongings of life and also death.
But not my compromise.

Printed in Great Britain
by Amazon